After All We Have Travelled

After All We Have Travelled

Sarala Estruch

Nine
Arches
Press

After All We Have Travelled
Sarala Estruch

ISBN: 978-1913437527
eISBN: 978-1913437534

Cover artwork: Zarina, 'Travels with Rani II,' 2008 (Woodcut on Okawara paper mounted on Arches cover buff paper). © Zarina; Courtesy of the artist and Luhring Augustine, New York. Photo: Farzad Owrang.

First published January 2023 by:

Nine Arches Press
Unit 14, Sir Frank Whittle Business Centre,
Great Central Way, Rugby.
CV21 3XH
United Kingdom

www.ninearchespress.com

Printed in the UK by Imprint Digital on recycled paper.

Nine Arches Press is supported using public funding by Arts Council England.

Supported using public funding by
ARTS COUNCIL ENGLAND

For my family

Contents

'The past continues to speak to us. But it no longer addresses us as a simple, factual "past", since our relation to it, like the child's relation to the mother, is always-already "after the break".'
– Stuart Hall

'What are the consequences of silence?'
– Bhanu Kapil

On Sound

They say no / sound

is ever lost / that

every wail / peal

of laughter / bullet

burst / every curse /

prayer / oath / every

water skim / pebble

roll / snail shell

crush / reverberates

indefinitely / at a

frequency / our ears

cannot touch / but

the body / hears

I

A Love Story, or The English Dream

London, 1976

do you remember / love / that day at the student hostel
on Cross Street / the way the light tilted in / at the window
to settle / on two emigrants / as we waited for our keys / except
now we'd arrived / we were emigrants no longer / but immigrants
carrying a larger suitcase / of connotations / me pale / skinned
in new flares / European features & / freshly bobbed hair / you
brown / skinned in polished oxfords / blazer & sleek side-parting /
that day the sunlight illuminated us equally / in love / as we were
with a country / gleaned from school textbooks & / photographs
your mother kept / in the album of her childhood // gardens
with rose bushes & / hedgerows / cherry-cheeked men / & women
chirping *good / morning* from behind / the garden gate /
neighbourly // it was not neighbourly / the way they looked
when you stepped on a bus or / the names / you were christened
at the restaurant where you worked / in the kitchen / suds up to
biceps / hands deep in the crud / of this country / washing &
washing / fingers still aching the following / morning as you took
notes in law school / while in the country of your birth / you'd dined
with nabobs / already received a bachelor's degree // these days
as we walk arm in / arm down London streets / turning our eyes &
ears inside out / to deflect stares & / curses / I recall the school
textbooks / manicured lawns / fences / & gates / cherry-cheeked
persons with wide open faces / & think *yes / the English are
neighbourly / as long as you stay / on your side of their gate*

Kesh (I)

kesh (from Punjabi keś) (noun) (mass noun): uncut hair worn as one of the
five Ks (the distinguishing signs of the Sikh Khalsa) by Sikh men and women

When one too many English women
crosses to the opposite pavement,
when he grows tired of mutterings
that trail him like the British clouds,
when the job interviews become
predictable and his landlord raises
the rent on his damp-infested flat
for the second time in six months,
he sharpens his blade, approaches
the mirror above the sink, the stink
of bleach and mildew rioting in
his nostrils, making his eyes smart
as he unravels the skeins of navy-
blue cotton, cloth falling away
from his head to reveal the black
glistening ocean beneath. As he
closes his fist around the rope,
he tries not to think of Biji or her
fingers washing, combing, plaiting
in the evenings of his childhood or
his father who taught him, on the
dawn of manhood, how to knot
a patka and tie a pagh so that if ever
a person were in trouble they would
see the turban and know to approach,
not turn their head in repulsion
as they did here in London in '73.
A prayer is lost somewhere between
tongue and teeth as he pulls the strands
taut as the strings of a sarod and brings
down the blade back and forth, back
and forth, witnesses the severance.

marry me

you bellow / the night
we stumble / into
your north / hackney flat

the air / between us
crackling / the dark
damp / staircase

lit / by truncated
flashes / here
inside / an emergency

of intimacy / skin
on skin / breath on
breath / hot Brut

& cigarettes / the
prickle of / yesterday's
stubble / our skin

in absence / of light
the same / shade
of night / fused

together / like layers
of cosmos / a soft
yielding / darkness

& through / that
darkness / we move
keep / on moving

tugging at / our
separateness / until
it is torn

Notes on Dreaming

There are times she closes
her eyes with him beside her and opens
to find him gone

with no idea of how or when
he left. There are times she sleeps so deeply
the room could be aflood

and she would not wake.
In these moments she is simultaneously
inhabiting the world

and escaping it – a toe, a heel,
an Achilles tendon in each realm: the material
and the unconscious

baring her weaknesses to all.

My Mother's Indian Wedding

My mother dreamt often of her Indian wedding,
of the house in Uttar Pradesh where it would take place –

with large adobe rooms and open lawns, a prayer room
on the roof, swathed in sun. A house she had seen

only once when visiting from England with my father –
surrounded by farmland: paddy fields and sugarcane;

beyond it, the jungle alive with swamp deer, rhino,
python, tiger. My mother dreamt of women in saris

and shalwars: silks of sindooram, cottons of sarason
woven with mirrors, knotted with gems, gold chains

trailing from ears, noses, necks; men in traditional Indian dress
or tailored suits and polished shoes, beards oiled,

turbans wrapped, shaking hands and pounding backs,
joking *Now the real work starts*. She dreamt of my father

in a gold-threaded kurta, chin and cheeks unshaven,
head bound in pink cloth; saw herself beside him,

swathed in flaming red, a chunni pulled over her crown
and forehead. She dreamt of the singing men who would chant,

over the harmonium and tabla, the words of the Guru Granth Sahib,
the sacred book she and my father would circle four times,

joined by a saffron-coloured scarf; his naked feet
as they stepped and hers following after. She could hear

their footfalls echoing one another, a tattoo of arches,
tendons and soles. She could feel the warmth of his body

radiating through his clothes, could almost smell the marigolds
around her neck, dripping their sweet demanding scent.

Between her fingers, the cloth chafed, sloughed off skin
but in the dream she gripped it firm. The thread held.

Starting from a Dream, 1983

Waking at night / My mother-to-be / approaches the window / hesitates / *in this foreign bed* / before the curtain / heart like a river / *with the wind running outside* / She finds lashings of rain / the sky clouded over / *as if it is being chased* / and strangely bright / The trees tremble / *and you in another bed* / She thinks of my father / a familiar stranger / *in another room* / since she arrived in this country and the faraway look / *on the other side* / his family wear whenever she enters a room / *of this ancestral kingdom* / as though they are already / watching her leave / *I am a spring* / The storm enters her / the brisk wind pushes her / *under a skin of soil* / against the glass of herself / and a part of her shatters / *a touch away from breaking* / while another rises / slips out into the urgent night / *through*

(Dis)Obedience

They said sever all ties. They said
forget her and the other her or him
that wasn't a her or him yet. It
was nothing. A tangled knot
undone. (*Thank god.*) Life goes on.

But it didn't. For you, life ended
when she fled the subcontinent
taking your mangled heart with her.
Breath continued, pull and tug
of lung, squeeze of bone on bone

inside your chest but you stopped
bathing, eating, seeing people.
Only slept. When your lids raised
you'd stare ahead at the white-
washed walls or the peeling ceiling

of your parents' home. They left
you alone, understood you needed
time. But time chased its tail and
caught it. Time came to take you
back to England, resume your work.

Weeks later they receive a phonecall
from the solicitor's office. You hadn't
shown up. When they call you
on the landline you don't pick up.
Your mother boards a plane,

arrives on a rainy September morning
at your flat in east London, pounds
on the door till her knuckles purple.
Eventually the landlord lets her in.
Pausing in the doorframe, she finds

you foetus-curled on top of sheets,
still wearing clothes she last saw
you in. She enters singing an old song
from the war days, tugs at the curtains.
Tepid sunlight invades your pillow.

She lugs the weight of you, the laggard
blood and bone of you, over her back
and right shoulder to the tub, scrubs
away the stink of folded flesh. She moves
into the kitchen, rudely awakens you

with the clank of pot on burner,
cloying stench of oats, milk and
sugar. Humming, she presses the cold
head of the spoon to your mouth
where it meets with barred teeth

over and over. Until one evening
you take the spoon and break
your vow of silence: *OK, Mum. Enough.*
She laughs aloud, throws her arms
round your shoulders, gives a little dance

then exits: *I have to call your father.*
Within days, you're waving
her off at Heathrow Departures.
Hours later, you call my mother,
ask to see us.

Photograph (I)

There is a photograph of me
perched on your shoulders

in a pastel pink duffel coat,
aged twelve months – or less

for my hair isn't proper hair yet
but tufts of downy fluff.

We've grins on our faces
as if there's only us

in this universe, which
(looking back) is apt

because they didn't know –
your other family,

the one you were born into –
they didn't know

how you'd grown into fatherhood
the way an orbit grows, ever expanding

and I didn't know
of your role as son, brother,

grandchild, nephew, cousin …
believing you were mine alone –

single star
in a sky I owned.

II

the things that remain

grey & blue   nike t-shirt
its confident tick   dissecting the chest

the dresses   he bought me
[pink & blue   candy-striped]

a pair of bedsheets   [ripped now
& faded   from over-use]

a pattern   of bulbous
smiling   sheep

two posters: the first
a painting of   lavender kittens

the second   a unicorn
standing   before a rainbow

as if expecting   to follow it
to   gold

The impermanence of things

is at times a relief

at other times intolerable

You know intimately

the fleeting nature of

tenderness   sparrows

hurtling towards a sky

that swallows them

After he died

you watched your mother

intricately lamented every

cough   sniffle

was certain that she too

would be taken

Wanting desperately

to own

something/someone

to have your share

you spun elaborate yarns

convincing

your younger (half) sister

that your mother

wasn't hers

After all

she still had her father

It was mathematical

One for you

one for her

My Indian Grandmother

Majestic with silver curls,
    like a taller version of the Queen,
she appears at my mother's flat
    six weeks after my father's death.
Call me Gran. I struggle to greet her.
    My father rarely mentioned her
or any family member. My mother
    shakes her hand with poise.
In the kitchen, the kettle screams.

She takes me shopping for the day.
    Have anything you like.
By the dress rack she is a million questions,
    wants to know my favourite
everything at the Pick N Mix aisle.
    I fill the paper bag at her insistence
with pear drops and marshmallow twists,
    don't tell her I'm not interested in things
I used to be: that liquorice doesn't taste
    as sweet, and red and green
have lost their radiance.

In the back of the taxi, I steal a closer look
    while her head's turned
absorbing London streets – regal neck
    and silver locks, pale skin
gently crêped. It's strange to think
    my father's hair will never grow white,
that his skin won't soften and fold
    into itself like a rose that holds
onto its stalk long after passing its peak.

Aerogramme (I)

Cerulean envelope falls through the letterbox –

untethered kite sinking in a windless sky

A letter folded into itself like origami

marked with tightly inked characters

The closing line *Please send her to us*

The first of many more to come

Mother-Daughter Conversations

And thus the litany begins:

'Your Indian family want
to see you; you must go to India
to meet them.'

'*I* must go? Not *we*?'
A derisive laugh.
'They're *your* family, not mine.'

She made it clear:
my father didn't belong to her.
I believed

they had separated
because they'd fallen
out of love

the way people do
because love is a cave –
or rather, a complicated

system of caves, a maze
of subterranean holes; alluring
darknesses to venture into

and scramble out of.

Freight

i

The art of packing light
is working out how much
of yourself you can leave

behind. Always keep
ample room for the desires
and expectations

others will pile up.
An empty rucksack that is
nevertheless

packed. A shell you were
born with – invisible yet
too weighty to bear.

ii

If a part of me
believed I was white; another
knew I wasn't.

I was raised in a
white home in a white
majority country

believing people
were praising the whiteness
in me when they called

me 'pretty'.
My chameleon skin
(platinum in snow

bronze in sun) meant
'passing' was a place to hide
the knowledge that I

could never be
beautiful like my (half) sister,
a real English rose.

iii

If there is one thing
I most want to take, it's my mother
but she won't come –

the blue aerogrammes
request me alone. This year
will be my first

Christmas and New Year's
without her. She asks for a model
of the Taj Mahal –

her miniature (bought
years ago at a bazaar)
has lost a minaret.

I hold the marble
sculpture in my hand and
imagine the country

that wants to claim me,
consider whether or not
I want to be claimed.

Home/Home

It is hard to feel Indian when this country is as unknown to you
        as you are to her. You want to get to know her, measure new sounds
on your tongue – Dadiji, Chachaji, Tayaji, Tayeeji – learn the infinite
        intricate ways you are connected to those around you: father's mother
(also father's father's sister), father's younger brother, father's
        older brother, father's older brother's wife ... Dadiji teaches you
what children here learn as infants: words for *water* ਪਾਣੀ
        and *breath* ਸਾਹ. Without ground for rooting, this new knowledge
flows in and out of you like ਪਾਣੀ, like ਸਾਹ. So she tells you again
        how to bend your knees, reach for the feet of elders to receive
their blessing; to cover your arms and legs; tilt your neck in demonstration
        of careful listening. When your grandfather leads you up the tangle of steps
to the prayer room, he gives you a scarf to place over your head
        for you own none that aren't thickly woven and those have been left
with the cold weather at home in England. Your grandmother
        keeps saying, like a mantra or affirmation that gathers conviction
on repetition, *This is your home. This is your home.*

Photograph (II)

It makes you feel special / the way they look at you / the way you are adored / by relatives who are unknown / to you but who loved your father / They want to touch you / Hands / shoulders / head / cheeks / Want to tell you / what a charming man he was / kind to everyone he met / Brilliant lawyer / top of his class / record-breaking athlete / heart of every social gathering / They scrutinise for semblances / lean in & question / mostly come up short / stating their conclusion / *You take after your mother* / But there is a photograph / on the wall of your grandparents' bedroom / your father as a young boy / smooth-cheeked / black hair tied back / large brown eyes set / on something out of frame / like looking at a past self / you had forgotten

Kesh (II)

i

I close my eyes to block sight of my hair
(some ten inches long) falling like wilted flowers,
hitting the ground neck-first.

Scissors keep gnashing and when at last
I lift my lids, the flowers are gone, replaced
by threshed wheat and all that remains

are golden seeds crowning my head.
I am nineteen years and eight hours old –
time to be shorn of the past.

ii

At home, mother opens the front door, lifts
her hands to her face, *Mon Dieu! What have
you done?* In the kitchen, her eyes are strobe

lights alternately flicking on the pot of lentils
she is stirring and my new short cut.
What will your grandparents think?

iii

The next morning, I begin to repent.
A glance at the calendar above my desk:
How much hair can you grow in three weeks?

I comb the slash of mane a thousand times
a day, hope tugging at roots will summon
growth. Too short to plait, a sharp-scissored trim

at a diagonal slant on full moon night
(guaranteed by mothers' law
to make hair grow back faster)

would, at this stage, only make matters worse.
Apprehensively, I prise the suitcase open,
fill its vacant mouth with scarves and hats.

iv

They love it. My Indian family say my short crop
makes me *smart*. Uncle proudly escorts me
to all the fashionable restaurants in Delhi, points out

a woman in a suit with a sleek brief bob then proceeds
to tell the story at all the dinner parties –
She looks just like the Modern Indian Woman!

v

My second-aunt (my father's cousin) gives me a gift
as if she isn't giving me a gift at all –
presses a gold chain into the flesh of my palm,

her face suddenly serious. *This is yours. It should have been
given to you at birth.* I smile and hug her, understanding
the gesture, not the words. Another second-aunt insists

on gifting me a pearl necklace. My first real pearls.
We didn't want to spoil you when you were younger.
My grandmother tugs at my arm, says it's time to get back.

The youngest second-aunt declares she won't be outdone
by her sisters. Insists on my following her up to the attic
although once we've vanquished the spiralling staircases,

she can't seem to find the box. While she searches, we talk.
Or rather, she talks and I listen. *I so admire your mother.*
After everything that happened, she still sends you here.

My aunt rises with a smile. *Found them! Close*
your eyes. A cold pinch on my left lobe, followed by
a colder pinch on the right. *Now. Open your eyes.*

vi

We only learn what we, in some way, already know.
Still, I'm not brave   enough to ask.
If I didn't talk much before, now I barely part my lips.

Listening becomes more than an art –
a mission. My ears spread.   Sure enough,
my grandmother starts to speak. I collect the words

like threads in a web that holds me, has held me
my entire life,   glittering lines of silk woven
in an intricate pattern I am only beginning to see –

He was always talking   about her   your mother
There were letters   She was   in each
blank   space   every   inked mark

39

the edible girl

'[I]f I didn't define myself for myself, I would be […] eaten alive'
 – Audre Lorde

i

i woke to find i was an edible girl   with heart of Deglet Nour
& brain of bitter gourd   limbs of barley   & ribs
of corn   teeth carved from coconut flesh   neck
wittled from sugarcane   feet of water   stomach of hollowed
casaba melon   sex of Sumoll   breasts of beet   lips
of stripped apple skin   hair of saag   boiled & stirred
into string   hands of Moraiolo olives   nails of almond
skin of squeezed marigold   & eyes stolen from the beating
chest of plum stones

ii

i gave my heart to my mother for she was hungry & unrequited
i gave my brain to my father for he was inspired & disillusioned

i gave my limbs to my stepfather for he was preoccupied with freedom
i gave my ribs to my sister to remind her to stand tall

i gave my teeth to my grandmother to create illusions of closeness & distance
i gave my neck to my grandfather to conjure the impression of height

i gave my feet to my uncle to ease his travel
i gave my stomach to my teachers & let them fill at will

i gave my sex to my lovers & breasts to the fashion industry
for they convinced me they owned them already

i gave my lips to co-workers & my hair to my friends
hands to all those i ever called employers

i gave up my nails to the government because they called them claws
i gave my skin to imperialists & my eyes to all the artists

who were so kind as to spit them back out but only once
they had been ground to dust

III

turtle

is it because he left
so suddenly & irrevocably
that i have lived my life
on land watching
collapse of water
a body rushes forward
in a curl of saline froth
then retreats –
there is the retreat
knowing this
each salted step
the careful equilibrium
me in me
–
of the sea
abandon our shells
kept as armour
& love

abandoned us
(twice)
as a sea creature
the slow rise &
the way
to embrace another
& desire
always
–
i measure with scales
not to crush
–
you in you
dinosaurs
we never completely
hard-boned carapaces
deflecting water
in equal measure

Aerogramme (II)

Blue envelope careens   through the letterbox –

dutiful dove, wrong-   hued, fluttering to

the *Welcome* mat   A letter folded

into itself   like a weeping child

knotted with blue-   inked characters

The closing line   *Please write –*

let us know   *you are okay*

how to talk about loss

'[B]ecause grief never leaves, it just changes shape'
 – Raymond Antrobus

how ~ after all these years
i still don't know ~

                                    where once was language
                                    now a lacking ~ void of sound ~

touch ~ absence ~ a mouth
drowned at high tide ~ for

                                    decades i've been a river-
                                    bed bereft ~ not a drop of

what i was made to hold ~
the thames has lessons to teach

                                    rain & me ~ forty-seven locks
                                    & weirs control the water ~

to make the river navigable ~
the thames tells me

                                    board a narrowboat ~ feel
                                    the body under you ~

its compact weight ~ its
liquid shape ~ adrift ~

                                    it's safe ~ try now ~ begin
                                    with facts ~ say he's gone ~

the lock gently
loosens ~ water trickles

later ~ say how ~ say
heart attack ~

the river flows higher ~
approaches the banks ~

once you practice the release
of jaw ~ the lift of tongue

of air from diaphragm ~
it gets easier ~ like a lock

frequently turned fends off rust ~
but ~ careful now ~ a lock

can snap ~ & if it does
the whole damn river

will arrive at once

The Measure of Water

Because my mother won't let me go to Indonesia
    to lose myself in relief work in the aftermath of the tsunami,
        I wind up here – Jamaica, March 2005 –
    being driven across the strip of land from Port Royal
to Kingston by Didi, a British expat who runs a school and
    wellbeing centre in the city. It is sunset, the water on either side
        of the road turning scarlet, as we drive towards an imposing rise
    she tells me is Blue Mountain, the island's highest peak.
When the road widens, Didi veers left, away from the mountain –
    we are no longer surrounded by sea but by buildings
        already too shrouded in shadow to be properly seen.
    By the time she points at a road, says *Down there's the school*
where you'll be working, it is ocean dark and the street
    trails off. She warns me not to dress in red or green
        on the days I work because the island is divided
    into two main gangs and Mountain View is the horizon
where sun and sea converge. *We are often forced to close the school.*
    I nod my understanding, promise I'll be careful.
        She continues, *You know, Port Royal was once the trading capital*
    of the New World, home to pirates and desperados
till 1692 when an earthquake shook the city and
    a tsunami followed, sucking buccaneers and bricks
        into the sea's belly. Part of the city still lies submerged.
    I listen closely as she tells of the Wickedest City in the World,
Captain Henry Morgan and company, and wonder
    why no mention of what brought these criminals to the island.
        Not liquor or sex workers but the white gold
    that hastens diabetes, fattens crowns, churns lives for profit.
Let's speak of this, too, I want to say, but don't. Not now,
    not yet. For who am I to ask such questions?

Blue Mountain

We had passed halfway point.
Every muscle in my body was singing,
brimming with lactic acid. We'd been arguing,
arguing as we climbed, about the best way
to climb a mountain, though I'd never climbed
a mountain before and you'd topped the summit
countless times. I wanted to enjoy the walk:
the winding path fringed with unfurling ferns
and bamboo stalks, gold and tall. You said:
To get to the top, you've got to look up.
Kept leading us off the path to the short cuts
through the underbrush over rocks and red soil.
Impossible to gain stable footing, we kept on
moving, the forward motion propelling us
a step ahead of stumbling. It started to rain.
You took my hand. The air thickened
with the scent of parched earth being pummeled
by water, particles of dust darting up, resisting
their muddy fate and already I was drenched,
had never been so wet; I'd never been so close
to the clouds with the rain coming down
and kept on going. At the summit we stood,
hearts swollen with victory and relief, though
thick grey mist had stolen the famous view
of the north and south coasts of the island.
Later, in the guesthouse in the valley,
you tell me of the Taíno and Maroons who
escaped slavery by fleeing to the Blue and
John Crow mountains; it was here, in unmapped
land colonists dared not enter, that they gathered,
grew strength, and planned their resistance.

To leap

'I didn't fall in love, I rose in it.'
  – Toni Morrison

       & not know

where you'll land – or even
if you will. I want to write

about hurling your heart,
blood & marrow against gravity,

pitching your strength
at every atom that has pressed

you down & soaring –
at least for a moment –

not knowing if that moment
will be eternity, a decade

or a breath's exhale. I want
to write about learning to live

with doubt, learning to rise in it;
learning to love like that.

Flight, or On Reading Ada Limón

There is so much living
we miss out on because of fear

like that plane we missed
by a millisecond because we

hesitated for a nanosecond
before stepping onto the escalator

or through the precarious doors
of the lift. & when I see us

standing here on the runway
of our lives as the jet flies

over our heads & the clock
tick tocks, impervious –

sometimes it's all I can do to stop
this vessel from self-combusting.

You want the truth? These poems
make me want to take life

by the neck & shake it up –
enough to tell us what we need

to know, how to race the clock
& overtake; leave time gasping

on the asphalt.

apparent stillwater

my body cannot be drawn
will not be still for even
the demi-semi-second it takes for
a shutter to close over
its form. even a lake moves
beneath the surface
though her face is impassive,
appearing impermeable –
so this rock sleeps
within my ocean and shifts
and shifts

An Inheritance

For Shivanee Ramlochan

A spirit hovered over the scene where the disobedience occurred
What kind of spirit   I couldn't tell   but it was there   trust me

as her lover leant over her sleeping body   & pressed his lips
to her neck & back   the crown of her silken tangled head

Outside the moon had risen & was slipping through the curtains
as a spirit watched a woman turn her sleep-heavy body

towards her lover   eyes still shut   as his hands touched   touched
& her skin rose   & the moonlight slipped inside

a bedroom   where there was no immaculate white   no unadult-
erated black   Tonight there were only adulterations

quarterons of light & dark   variations on a variegated spectrum
of in-betweens   & this released them   The spirit watched

as they   man & woman   swam in infinite spectra of indefinition
until they sank   & having sunk   resurfaced   gasped for breath

elation   the terrible orgasmic thrill of creation   stroking their
flanks   reverberating in their bones   the knowingness of cells

having made an image of themselves inside her   A miniature
or photograph   Proof of the breaking

of unwritten rules of state   & above all   his parents' wishes
In that moment the spirit upped & left   vanished into nothing

or maybe something   no one knows for certain but I have an idea
You see   the image grew   It grew & grew until it had a mouth

nose   cheeks &   eyes   with which to survey grandparents &
state   & when the image was born   the story goes

that through the tears of newborn wails   though it was
impossible   the baby / spirit-child arose

Us

Eating, sleeping, washing and loving –
this is all we do for days and months.

No speaking – we develop a new language
of facial expressions, sound, touch.

When you weep, I press your body to my chest –
heat evaporates and crystals form,

multiply until there has grown
an entire forest of salted consolation.

Night and day are borderless –
I half-sleep listening for your butterfly breath.

Our dreams are full of colour and wordless song.
For us, melody is enough.

I love everything about being a mother

I said   before I remembered   the days
when my teeth   went unbrushed   &
the way   he screamed   when I placed
him on   the bathroom floor   to take
a shower   at four   in the afternoon
Days when   I have   done nothing
but   breastfeed   &   breastfeed   &
wipe   turmeric curdles   from his tiny
rump   How   after a week   of not
washing   not combing   my hair   hung
in a rope   at the nape   of my neck
bound   like a loaf   of bread   Nights
when I was lucky   to close   my eyes
for fifteen   minutes   Mornings
when the face   in the mirror   is pale
linen   stre t ch ed   o v er   the rack
of me   blustering   in a careless wind

Woman, Saint, (M)Other

I was never less ready for motherhood than this moment:
standing in front of my six-year-old son and he suddenly
so inquisitive, asking who God is and why people die.
I can only answer honestly *I don't know* and I see disappointment
on his face, bright as colostrum.

                    The bad mother (more Magdalene
than saint), I haven't mastered the art of meditation or eternal
optimism; samadhi having persistently eluded me, my mind is a rover
wandering where it shouldn't, over mountains or into dark cramped
caves – I struggle sometimes to pull myself out.

                          I say none of this
to him though he notes the sighs, frequent dampness of cheek. Child,
please don't see these as signs of lack of love. If love could be measured
in exhales, I would be breathless. I promise I want nothing more
than to rejoice in every cell of your being (extraordinary, mediocre and
imperfect) but, rogue teacher that I am, I have still so much to learn.

The Gorge

Red ochre squelching underfoot, holding
onto her soles then relenting: letting go.
She walks into the deep green not knowing
which way but not wanting to turn back.
The canvas of green & red blurring her edges,
making her reckless. Except. The granite sky.
The wind whipping hard. Her shoes ravaged
by mud. She finds herself in a gorge: ripe,
overflowing, the water tumbling from wet
hand to wet hand, creating a dozen fresh
water paths. Her foot sticks. Another step
& her foot sinks half a metre into the soil.
A rustling in the leaves from the trees on
her right & the fear (never far away) returns:
of being found. *By whom?* She doesn't know
but the cold knife slicing through her
abdomen is real. Terror cuts to her lungs,
the red ochre in her veins runs to her heart
& flees again, disperses into valves, capillaries.
She breathes in red & green as her feet
pummel the soil, travel the water-paths carved
in the earth's skin. This was what she had
wanted (to be alone) but not *this*: the crack
& recoil of thunder as gunshot, her heart
punishing her chest. She wishes she had done
something useful with her youth like learn
a martial art. Her youth now almost gone.
Thirty-four – not young, not old. Somewhere
in between. She turns back to the trees.
Here is a path she recognises; this ditch,
this hassock. It is not the path she'd planned
on taking but she takes it now. Appearing
at the front door, mud up to her shins;
flushed, smiling. *I took the long way back.*

IV

Return

No more stepping from the loins of the silver bird
into the hot, breathy mouth of India. The single step
through the plane's open door leads to a tunnel
identical to the one we stepped into eleven hours ago
at Heathrow. Grey-carpeted, white plastic walls
on all sides, a canal birthing us into the womb of
Indira Gandhi International Airport. The man
at immigration peers at us, our children; asks
for passports, visas, forms. We fumble, fingers drowsy
after flight. In crossing half the world, we've lost a night,
the almost-noon Delhi sun tumbling through skylights.
He shuffles papers. Sweat pearls my upper lip.
Why do I suddenly feel like a fraud? He enunciates
my name the way Indians do, with a hard rolling 'r'
I can't replicate. 'Yes. My father was Indian.'
He is incredulous. 'And where is your husband from?'
'Jamaica.' The immigration man is half-amused,
half-bemused. 'The children are *very* mixed,' I grin.
'They are universal,' the officer says, handing us
our papers. The gate opens, and the room is shining,
sunlight scuttling off the white floor, walls, our broad smiles.
My husband takes our son's hand, I take our daughter's.

To Make Him Real

'I remember […] which is to say I am putting it together.'
– Ocean Vuong

There was always a distance between us.
We never lived together, didn't slumber
under the same roof. A visiting daughter,
I called him by his first name. Listen how
I call you 'him' because I'm too afraid
to address you, father. *Father*. So formal.
Fear makes me formal. And again I am
talking about me when it's you I need
to remember. Your broad, raised nose.
Your mischievous smile. Your voice
which I've taken too long to elegise
and so forgotten. Your six-foot silhouette
is fading, stepping into shadow. Your
sideways parting. Your polo shirts.

Grandmother, Dreaming

In my grandparents' bedroom, bathed in sunset's crimson light, my grandmother is dreaming. She lies beneath two or three thick razai woven with a single flower pattern repeated like waves on the ocean or the way a body breathes. Her body, under blankets, is a trickle of water evaporating and there is nothing she or I can do. She jokes about how the cancer has made her high-fashion material. Says *Vogue* will headhunt her now. Of course this is all decades too late. She is 81 years old. The only things her stomach will accept are a square or two of her favourite Cadbury's and the rainbow of pills she swallows daily. She wants to please. Tries the homeopathic remedies my mother has sent. Keeps saying how much better a woman my mother was than my father's eventual wife. I wonder what my grandmother dreams beneath the patterned waves. Maybe she is dreaming of the day my father was born. In her dream, she can still hold him, his chest rising and falling against hers. I hope she does not dream of his death. When she wakes, she will tell me forbidding my parent's marriage is the biggest regret of her life. It is also mine, though I don't say it. I will give forgiveness when she asks.

Dear Father

Tonight we arrived at the family home. It was dark. We stepped through the meshed screen into the tiled entrance to find the stuffed swamp deer, antlered and black-eyed, relic from your hunting days. Grandad in the living room, switching off the television. I introduced him to my husband and children – your grandchildren. I wish you could have seen how his smile embraced us. How he looked strong as nine years ago, only his hair was milk-white. Strange as it is to write, there is something of you here now. Gran too. These rooms pulse with you, motes of thought and feeling still in motion; the way a person lingers in the fabric of carpets, the plaster of walls, long after they have left. It feels so good to have arrived home – by which I mean, I have belonged here once, perhaps I can belong here again.

Bouchon

My first word, according to my mother,
in my first language. French for bottleneck,
cork, plug, stopper. Referring, she says,
to the bottle of nappy cream she'd use
when changing me. A playground of sound:
bouncing *buh* chased by a persistent *oo,*
gusty whoosh and brusque nasal break.
Surprising, really, that it wasn't 'Maman'
though perhaps it was and she has forgotten.
Instead, she has chosen to remember
my connection with language as a stopper
and it's true, sometimes I fear the cost:
how it holds things down. Its false claim
to ownership. And I think of all the nameless
things a poet spends her life chasing and
never quite arriving at. Here in the land
of my father and my father's father, I know
so little my hungry mind gorges, fed to
bursting. There are no stoppers –

Anand Karaj

After Kayo Chingonyi

Since my parents did not circle the Guru Granth Sahib
as holy men sing songs of union with God, did not
receive semolina sweets or the blessings of my father's
relatives, I know nothing of Indian wedding traditions.
I wear white to my uncle's engagement, not knowing
white is the colour of funerals; my ears carry costume
jewellery where only real silver or gold will do.

This is all so new. Dupattas intricately wrapped,
saris draped and tucked. I have never seen so many
shades of pink, a plethora of tiny square-mirrors stitched
with matching embroidery. My aunt-to-be takes me
under her wing, helps me pick out cloth for the wedding:
fuchsia for the Anand Karaj, midnight blue for the
reception. The tailor carefully measures my shape.

If I were to meet her – that alternate self, born of a union
blessed – what would she make of me, awkward and
struggling to speak, here in our father's land? I, who
call England my home, which is also our father's land.
Would it be visible: how much more she measures here
than me? Or would she smile, take my hand, and
would we pace, in our parents' place, around the book?

I research the origins of the modern rose & discover

1. she is a crossbreed

2. of *Rosa chinensis, Rosa gigantea* & other species

3. including *Rosa gallica* & *Rosa canina*

4. of which, only the latter, is native to the British Isles

5. the rest were shipped from China, India, France

6. et cetera, et cetera …

7. Flower with a thousand faces, six thousand five hundred tongues

8. & almost as many names;

9. ancestors estimated at thirty-five million years old.

10. To where does she return?

11. She becomes what she is:

12. 玫瑰, गुलाब, *rose.*

The Residency, Lucknow

The morning you visit The Residency, the April sun is already high
and intolerable; a brightness blearing the information plaques.

Crumbling walls pierced with exit wounds. There is no guide
to talk you through who owned and lived in which derelict pile

or lead you to the museum (which you discover, on return
to England, is a highlight). Only your cousin and husband,

both dehydrated, and the children who must be kept out of the sun
as much as possible. This is impossible. You almost give up,

sitting in shade of a tree with a name you don't know
in front of another ruin, history unforthcoming; a legend written

in script you can't read. You want to understand this, want
and – at the same time – don't want to know the truth

about what happened here. The hurt inflicted on your ancestors
on both sides from both sides. This is your inheritance –

or at least a part. You are here now; living, breathing
                                                question mark.

Vaisakhi, *Vaisakhi*

Vaisakhi is a spring festival celebrated throughout India and the world.
Britain still hasn't formally apologised for the Jallianwala Bagh massacre
which took place in Amritsar on Vaisakhi in 1919.

14 April 2019

On the morning of Vaisakhi
we rise and, after breakfast,
dress our heads in cotton cloth
climb the white stone staircase
to Grandfather's prayer room

On the roof, we remove
our shoes and step into
the glass-panelled room
bowing before the sacred book
as Uncle has shown us

Grandfather is already there
sat behind the Guru Granth Sahib
draped in gold gossamer
he pulls away The children watch
in silence The children wait

Grandfather opens the book
at random, begins to read and
we listen, understanding not
with our ears but with our hearts:
a lord's prayer on this auspicious day

When he is finished, he reads
another prayer just for us
which he translates line by line
thanking God for our safe arrival
blessing our golden lives

13 April 1919

On the morning of Vaisakhi
we rise and, after breakfast,
dress in our finest, travel to
Jallianwala Bagh and gather
with family and friends

In full sunlight, we sit
on packed earth, spread
the cloth, lay out food
We thank God for the meal
bring rice and dal to our mouths

The soldiers are already there:
standing on the mount, guns raised
Bullets burst Bodies tumble
to the earth The children watch
in silence The children wait

Then they run, we all run –
there is nowhere to go Bullets
pummelling the single exit
which is also the single entrance
Some of us jump into the well –

We who survive utter prayers
for those we lost The time
has passed for screaming; the time
is ripe for grieving For apology
Atonement Healing

Grandfather Speaks (via Audio Recording)

'[T]he family story. Is it there for the taking?
[...] Is it mine for the taking?'
Moniza Alvi

'Partition was surely more than just a political divide ... It was also,
to use a phrase that survivors use repeatedly, a "division of hearts".'
Urvashi Butalia

Winter 1952. Three years and stepping off the train
   he'd forgotten the sting of the Bristolian wind,
      having traversed seas and oceans to ask my future
   grandmother for her hand in marriage. After months
of airmail letters, her answer is already sealed.
   Back home, he'd had his work cut out, scything
      grasses, clearing jungle to make home and farm
   for his widowed mother, younger brother and future wife.
He speaks with pride of how he baked each brick,
   doesn't say why – at 21 – he had to start from mud
      when his father had been a surgeon. Doesn't mention
   the other family home abandoned overnight
in that other country which had once been
   the same country. Doesn't say   disjuncture
      rupture   severance.   Doesn't say:
trauma   of body   mind
heart.   Doesn't say   Punjab.
   After all we have travelled   Grandfather doesn't speak
      of the things he believes he's left behind and
   I've inherited. When a favourite poet says be shameless
about your shame, he means this moment. He means
   me sitting with my grandfather's unspoken words
      in my ear and willing him to say them, though I know
   these words can never be spoken – not by him –
speaking as he is from the other side of life.

Camera Lucida

After Roland Barthes

I – [Specialty of the Father]

I wasn't sure that [my father] *existed*

II – [The Father Unclassifiable]

[Lost fathers are] *unclassifiable […] / deprived of a principle of marking*

III – [The Father Unclassifiable II]

Who could help me?

IV – [Father as Departure]

I looked for him in people –

his mother   his father   his brother
myself

But *from the first step*   and at every step
[Father] *evades us*

V – [Father as Departure II]

Not here [Not here] Not here either

VI – [This Fatality]

No [lost fathers] *without* **something** *or* **someone** /
[a son or daughter / a child left behind] /
involves [lost fathers] *in the vast disorder of objects*

VII – [Father as Interrogation]

I searched for him in things   the house where he grew up
tall mahogany furniture   humidity-bound books   airmail
letters disintegrating in corners   photographs …

VIII – [He Who Photographs]

Photograph pasted on the final page
of my father's album –
the one he was compiling
when he died

[following several empty pages]

[Portrait of a Rose]

The flower   is falling
into itself   petals imploding
red disaster   on a stalk
of deep green thorns   standing
intact –   the soft parts
are always   first to fade

IX – [Camera Lucida]

closer, even –
zoomed in   The photograph stuns me

I am looking at [a rose through the] *eyes* [of my father]

– the closest I have been to him in decades

X – [Specialty of the Father II]

[O]f all the objects in the world
why choose   (why photograph)
this object   this moment
rather than some other?

And in this manner?

XI – [Punctum: Partial Feature]

I know the rose / is red when to the eye / it is
only a whorl of greys / against a sheet of whites /
This photograph wounds me / marks my heart
with its pointed instruments / of light and shade /
It is this play / of bright and dark / encroachment
of the melancholy which held him / the last years
of his life / Did he already miss me then /
though living / the way I miss him now

XII – [After-the-Fact and Silence]

*Whatever it grants to vision and whatever
its manner / a* [lost father] *is always invisible /
it is not it that we see*

Ghazal: Say

After Will Harris

There is *no definable point at which a living organism dies*, scientists say.
It shakes me to read words I've been striving all these years to find, to say.

The universe is rarely ordered in binary ways. How to articulate this
basic and profound truth my mind struggles to believe, let alone say?

All I know is you've been gone these long years and, at the same time, you haven't,
you've been right here, though, till now, it's not something I thought I could say.

'Dead' and 'alive' are terms *whose meanings are wholly psychological.*
Physiochemically [...they] merge into one another. They bleed, you could say.

Bleed the way my knee did, releasing its dark stain; running too fast to meet you
I fall, and what was once inside me now on your hands, your blue shirt. Sorry, I say.

You pull me close. In the garden beside the alley in which we crouch,
the chestnut trees are whispering, a sound only half got out. Sorry, you say.

The whispering grows louder, reverberates in my ear, my throat.
Father, and Poet. Tell me honestly. What are you – what am I – trying to say?

Notes

Opening epigraphs are from Stuart Hall's essay 'Cultural Identity and Diaspora', which appears in *Identity: Community, Culture, Difference* edited by Jonathan Rutherford (Lawrence Wishart, 1990) and Bhanu Kapil's *The Vertical Interrogation of Strangers* (Kelsey Street Press, 2001).

'I research the origins of the modern rose & discover' was written, in part, as a response to then Prime Minister Theresa May's comment in 2016: *'If you believe you are a citizen of the world, you are a citizen of nowhere'*. The last three words of the poem repeat the word 'rose' in three languages: Mandarin, Hindi, and French.

In 'Ghazal: Say', italicised words are quotations from 'The Map of Four Kisses', an essay by Nuar Alsadir which was published in *The Poetry Review*, 109:2, Summer 2019. The first and third quotations are the words of psychoanalyst Charles Brenner. The second quotation consists of Alsadir's words.

Acknowledgements

Thank you to Arts Council England for awarding me a Developing Your Creative Practice grant in 2018. Many of these poems were researched and began (in some way) during the period of development their financial support offered me.

Thank you to the other arts organisations who have supported me and the writing of this book, especially the Poetry School.

Special thanks to Jacob Sam-La Rose, Nii Ayikwei Parkes, and the team at flipped eye for first publishing several of these poems in my debut pamphlet *Say* (2021).

Thank you to the editors of the following publications, where some of these poems have previously appeared (often in earlier versions): *Primers: Volume Three* (Nine Arches Press), *Islands Are But Mountains: New Poetry from the United Kingdom* (Platypus Press), *amberflora, Out of Time: Poetry from the Climate Emergency* (Valley Press), *MIR Online, harana poetry, Tomorrow* (Creative Future), *The Poetry Review, Under the Radar, How It Started* (Creative Future), *Poetry Birmingham Literary Journal, Poetry Wales,* and *Wild Court.*

Thank you to the late artist and printmaker Zarina and to her estate for giving me permission to use the beautiful artwork on the front cover. 'Travels with Rani II' resonates with this book in so many ways.

A heartfelt thank you to all my teachers and mentors, especially Sarah Howe, Sandeep Parmar, Jacob Sam-La Rose, Mimi Khalvati, Nick Makoha, Hannah Lowe, Martina Evans, Melanie Abrahams, Jack Underwood, Shivanee Ramlochan, and Mona Arshi. Your support and belief in my work made this book possible.

Enormous thanks to Jane Commane for believing in my work all these years and for all the hard work you have put into making this book a reality. Your vision for Nine Arches is so inspiring and I am proud to be a part of the Nine Arches family. Massive thanks also to Angela Hicken, marketing marvel.

To the Ledbury Poetry Critics and mentors — thank you. I am honoured to belong to a network of such talented and inspiring people.

For friendship, support, and encouragement: thank you to my Kinara sisters (Anita Pati, Gita Ralleigh, Rushika Wick, and Shash Trevett), Mary Jean Chan, Srishti Krishnamoorthy-Cavell, Maryam Hessavi, Mónica Parle, Jennifer Wong, Jennifer Lee Tsai, Victoria Aduwkei Bulley, Lesley Sharpe, and Dave Wakely.

To my non-writer friends who have kept me (sort of) sane over the years – Sushila, Ida, Ayesha, Tara, and Irina. Thank you for your friendship, support, and understanding.

Thank you to my mum, my sister, and my family around the world for understanding the importance of literature in my life and the wider world.

A million thanks to Aaron, Alex, and Tara for being the biggest supporters of my work and the shining lights in my life.

And finally, thank you to all the poets and readers of poetry who keep poetry alive and relevant to our lives.